A test of love

And the way to grow in oneness

Is to share deeply

And discuss openly

All that concerns us

With acceptance

And appreciation.

Talking It Over

John M. Drescher
Introduction by
Clayton C. Barbeau

HERALD PRESS
Scottdale, Pennsylvania
Kitchener, Ontario

Dedicated
to those couples
who take the necessary time
to enlarge their understanding and appreciation
of each other through the use
of this booklet.

AUTHOR'S PREFACE

Talking It Over grew out of a great deal of testing in many husband-wife retreats and counseling situations. The idea of such a booklet was stimulated initially by my seeing the booklet *Dyadic Encounter* published by University Association Press.

Talking It Over was initially tested in mimeographed form, given to couples to work through after several sessions in a retreat or in counseling. Even husbands and wives whose children were grown expressed appreciation for its use.

Some couples spent as many as seven to eight hours discussing these open-ended questions. They report that they have learned to know and appreciate each other in numerous new ways after thirty or more years of marriage.

It would, of course, be ideal if couples could work through the booklet during the first year of marriage.

Talking It Over has many uses — in retreat settings, as an exercise in informal husband and wife group discussions, as follow-up of counseling sessions, and simply to give a couple after some months of marriage.

John M. Drescher
Scottdale, Pennsylvania

INTRODUCTION

When I first discovered *Talking It Over*, I recognized it as one of those deceptively simple instruments capable of accomplishing considerable good when properly used.

My own work with married couples involves fostering enrichment of the husband-wife relationship through exercises designed to help them achieve a higher level of intimacy in communication. Since discovering this book, I have provided it to the couples in my seminars, given it as "homework" for them, and also introduced it to clergy looking for means to help couples improve their conjugal dialogue.

One priest has written me: "I've put my copy to use with a couple. It's wonderful." Couples have informed me that it has opened new doors for them in their appreciation of each other.

In the last twenty years of involvement in family life work, I have become convinced that honest dialogue between husband and wife is the vital ingredient of a living marriage. Without it we get those "marriages of strangers," those "stale-mated" situations that are so common.

Our human need for being understood and accepted by others, especially by those with whom we share our lives, is so easily deprived of necessary sustenance. It is so often hard to express our true feelings, to come to terms with them. How easy, how much less risky, to lapse into routines that are functional and superficial. We can use business or busy-ness to fill the days, talk about things, or the children, or what's on TV, or problems at the job as dodges to avoid talking about what really matters — how we feel about ourselves and our relationship.

So often I hear couples say they just can't seem to "find time" to discuss their relationship. I advise them that time is not "found." I have yet to meet anyone who has spotted thirty minutes or stumbled across an hour while he was walking along the path to work. No, time is created by us. We make time. What we make time for speaks eloquently of what is important to us.

If we create some time to be with one another to use this booklet in the hopes that it will enhance our relationship, we have already communicated something of great value to each other. We've said that our relationship is important to us, that it is worth our time. We have also said that the other is important to us, that what the other thinks and feels is of concern to us.

John Drescher has informed me that anyone who goes through this booklet in an hour is not communicating. I agree wholeheartedly. This is not a volume to be read, nor an exercise to complete in a series of quick responses. It is a tool which permits a couple of travel at their own speed and level of comfort. But that speed should be a thoughtful, relaxed pace. The couples who will get the most out of the exercise will be those who take their time, who meditate upon the opening lines, get in touch with their most honest feelings, memories, thoughts, and only then seek to form the words that give expression to the movements of the spirit.

We live in an era of "encounter groups" and "sensitivity sessions." The true "encounter group," the authentic "sensitivity workshop," is the family. There it is that we are meant, by sharing ourselves, to become more truly human, accepting and accepted for ourselves.

Our union in love, by virtue of our humanity, is always incomplete in this life. We are mysteries even to ourselves. There is no day on which I can say I know another person — even the one to whom I am married — completely. Each marriage partner is an absolutely unique person and therefore a mystery never to be exhausted of meaning. Our intimacy with each other is an ongoing thing, our union with each other a creative labor of love which offers us, almost daily, new insights into one another and ourselves.

Intimacy in marriage is not automatic. It is always in need of nurturing, in need of attention, if it is to grow. *Talking It Over* becomes an easy doorway for us to enter into meaningful encounter. However healthy we deem our marriage, setting aside time to be with one another and use this book may be just the occasion of grace our marriage needs at this moment.

Talking It Over may be just the communications instrument you need to bring new life, new insight, improved understanding to your relationship. To my mind, there is no marriage, however healthy, that cannot benefit from *Talking It Over*.

Clayton C. Barbeau, Author
Living Marriage: Alternative to Divorce

HOW TO USE THIS BOOK

Relationships in marriage grow and mature only as we let our partner know how we think and feel. And to learn to know one another means self-disclosure, self-awareness, nonpossessive caring, risk-taking, acceptance, feedback, and honesty.

When this happens the result is greater feelings of trust and love and all our relationships are blessed.

These discussion items are open-ended. They can be completed at whatever level of self-disclosure is desired. It is better to discuss ten pages in depth than all the pages in a hurried fashion without really communicating.

The pattern is simple. A couple must be alone, away from distractions. Take one page at a time. Do not look ahead. Each partner should respond to each statement before continuing. Take turns in leading out. At the back, turn the booklet upside down and work toward the front.

Continue on other subjects if you wish, or go back and discuss anything you feel further need to talk about.

Right now I'm feeling . . .

If we don't . . .

Our backgrounds are . . .

Where we must start is . . .

The relation of my parents to each
  other was . . .

I think what we ought to do is . . .

My childhood home atmosphere was . . .

I would like you to . . .

74

Sharing intimate things with my
parents was . . .

What I think you ought to know is . . .

(Response to and acceptance of others depends a lot on how one feels about oneself.)

I think I am . . .

(Here share honestly what you think about yourself.)

Right now this experience is making
me feel . . .

I think other people think I am . . .

A discussion of sex usually . . .

I feel God thinks I am . . .

Right now I'm most reluctant to discuss . . .

Three things which attracted me to
you were . . .

The thing I feel strengthens our relationship most is . . .

My reaction when I feel I am misunderstood is . . .

When I think about the future I . . .

(Here the first speaker should answer in
 two or three sentences.
The second should say, "If I hear what
 you are saying it is . . ." and repeat
 to the other's satisfaction.
Reverse the process. Are you a good
 listener?)

The thing which turns me off most is . . .

My feelings toward your parents are . . .

I find it difficult to give myself when . . .

Check yourself here.
   Am I listening?
   Am I being honest?
   Am I comfortable or uptight?
   Am I trusting you?

Our love is different than in courtship.
Now it is . . .

I am happiest when . . .

The time I feel closest to you is . . .

At times I feel lonely because . . .

I wish I would not need to . . .

Do I feel free to discuss anything
with you? . . .

When you are gone I feel . . .

In order to live happily together I believe husband and wife must . . .

The greatest hindrance to our happiness, I feel, has been . . .

I anticipated marriage would be . . .

When I hear of friends whose marriage is
breaking up I . . .

The time I find it easiest to talk is . . .

The points at which I feel we are quite
  different are . . .

The happy time together that I remember most is . . .

These differences have . . .

Right now our love relationship is . . .

Our marriage has been . . .

Do something to express how you feel toward the other without words . . .

Toward you right now I feel . . .

Saying thank you, pardon me, please, I'm sorry, and forgive me is . . .

When a serious problem arises between us I usually react by . . .

I wish we together could . . .

My deepest fears are about . . .

To me, taking orders from another
person is . . .

Sometimes I wish you would . . .

In money matters I feel we . . .

The emotion I feel most difficult to control is . . .

I am most ashamed of . . .

My most frequent daydreams are about . . .

I believe I can im _ _ _ e in . . . .

When I feel rejected I . . .

You expect me to . . .

What I appreciate most about you is . . .

I experience the best sex satisfaction
   when . . .

One thing which hurts down deep yet I've never shared with you is . . .

I feel most affectionate when . . .

Turn booklet upside down to continue on page 47.

John M. Drescher is pastor of the Scottdale Mennonite Church, Scottdale, Pennsylvania. From 1962 to 1973 he edited *Gospel Herald*, the official weekly magazine of the Mennonite Church. He served on the board of Associated Church Press.

Drescher's articles have appeared in approximately one hundred magazines and journals. Much of his writing has been in the area of family. He is the author of *Meditations for the Newly Married, Now Is the Time to Love, Follow Me, Heartbeats, Spirit Fruit,* and a series of eleven Visitation Pamphlets.

John and his wife, Betty, have held numerous family and married couples' retreats throughout North America. He served on the planning committee of the Continental Congress on the Family held in St. Louis in October 1975.

The Dreschers are parents of three boys and two girls: Ronald, Sandra, Rose, Joseph, and David. Family hobbies include music, crafts, camping, clocks, and gardening.